W9-BBL-938

3 4028 09048 5120
HARRIS COUNTY PUBLIC LIBRARY

811.6 Jac
Jackson, Major
Roll deep : poems

$26.95
ocn891611181
First edition.

Roll Deep

ALSO BY MAJOR JACKSON

Holding Company

Hoops

Leaving Saturn

Roll Deep

POEMS

MAJOR JACKSON

W. W. NORTON & COMPANY

NEW YORK • LONDON

Copyright © 2015 by Major Jackson

All rights reserved
Printed in the United States of America
First Edition

For information about permission to reproduce selections from this book,
write to Permissions, W. W. Norton & Company, Inc.,
500 Fifth Avenue, New York, NY 10110

For information about special discounts for bulk purchases, please contact
W. W. Norton Special Sales at specialsales@wwnorton.com or 800-233-4830

Manufacturing by Courier Westford
Book design by JAM Design
Production manager: Louise Mattarelliano

Library of Congress Cataloging-in-Publication Data
Jackson, Major, 1968–
[Poems. Selections]
Roll deep : poems / Major Jackson. — First edition.
pages ; cm
ISBN 978-0-393-24689-6 (hardcover)
I. Title.
PS3610.A354A6 2015
811'.6—dc23
2015009527

W. W. Norton & Company, Inc.
500 Fifth Avenue, New York, N.Y. 10110
www.wwnorton.com

W. W. Norton & Company Ltd.
Castle House, 75/76 Wells Street, London W1T 3QT

1 2 3 4 5 6 7 8 9 0

FOR DIDI JACKSON

CONTENTS

9

ACKNOWLEDGMENTS

I wish to thank the editors of the following publications for gathering an early audience for these poems: the Academy of American Poets' *Poem-A-Day*, *Best American Poetry 2013*, *Best American Poetry 2014*, *The Café Review*, *Callaloo*, *The Common*, *Harpur Palate*, *Little Star*, *New Letters*, *The New Republic*, *The New York Times Style Magazine*, *The New Yorker*, *The Paris Review*, *Ploughshares*, *Plume*, *Solstice Literary Magazine*, *Tin House*, *Virginia Quarterly Review*, and *Washington Square*. Some of these poems appear in the chapbook *The Sweet Hurried Trip Under an Overcast Sky* by Floating Wolf Quarterly.

My crew rolls deep, too numerous to name here. Gratitude and praise is owed to the global village of poets, intellectuals, artists, culture workers, peace lovers, earth stewards, music makers, and thought boosters. Your brilliance inspires and your conversations ignite fires in the brain. I also wish to thank Christopher Merrill and Kelly Bedeian of International Writing Programs at the University of Iowa for the opportunity to travel to Kenya as part of *Reading Abroad: American Writers on Tour*. Once again, I am grateful for the guidance and support of my editor Jill Bialosky who inspires by example as literary artist and discerning reader.

This book was written while on fellowship from the Guggenheim Foundation to whom I express immense gratitude.

Finally, many of these poems would not have been written were it not for the support, belief, editorial suggestions, and straight-up inspiration of my wife and life-mate Didi Jackson. To her and our family: Langston, Anastasia, Dylan, and Romie; your love, in the end, is all that matters. Thanks for showing me the ropes and keeping me laughing.

Roll Deep

One

My soul has grown deep like the rivers.

—LANGSTON HUGHES

REVERSE VOYAGE

My midway journey, my emancipated eyes
like runaways, exposed, and the row homes stacked
again, colorless drab LEGO blocks. I come
back to unlit alleys, avenues in sheaths of grit
and utility wires like veins stitched to power supplies
buzzing above a different kind of hum.
Just when my seeing was rectifying into
something faultless, extraordinary as a cat's refuge
beneath a parked car, I'm brought back to
the silence, oblique, hidden deep inside
the ventricle caves of my body's chambers,
to nail salons, check cashing stores, pawnshops.
How characteristic of them to greet me though,
the old folk, in such a way: magisterial.
The corner store with its faded graffiti lines,
finally whitewashed, nearly expunged,
doubtless like its author save for his palimpsest,
and yet, behind a first-floor window, a young boy bends
over an old encyclopedia, a remarkable script,
a genuine compendium that shows his people's Africa
like a sculpted mask for tourists in an open-market
which he slowly turns contemplating skin, the color
of almonds, pyramids, revolutions, and other such beauties.
Human strength never before seen kept those
mystical relations alive until they touched themselves
again, revived songs albeit injured, but no less rich.
Even here, all's remixed. In Fairmount Park,
a posse plays the same din with fresher strains

of freedom, what never passes. That is the message,
always, of its august lines, a rangy dignity,
the lesson, too, of what one refuses to never forget
about this place: a grandmother, Mrs. Pearl, a domestic,
thirty years boarding SEPTA early mornings.
I think of her, clutching a tan purse, statelier than these lines.
So oblivion vacates memory—these connecting
columns of bricks, and wires, and me, its last deportee
which the blood sings no matter snowcaps,
no matter mountainous ranges and glittering lakes
like flashing daggers, no matter allegory of hoarfrost,
no matter tractor parades and morning
finches and bluejays that skitter my sight in a valley
far away from city pigeons who hop and settle off electric
wires near street gutters to peck heads at one crumb
or another, where local inhabitants, too, study skies
with a certainty affixed to rooftops and flashing
underbelly green & red lights going elsewhere or nowhere.
The city's skyscrapers tower: a retired bricklayer
and his wife, the old folk, locked in a grid of streets and their
still-standing three-story on a strip of mostly weed-laden lots,
like a tore-up mouth, where their minds recall,
for sixty years, just where to lay a hand on a railing
& then the stairs that not long ago led up to you or me.
The white marbled steps and boarded-up doorways
and basement windows spilling out debris and rusted springs,
say *Return to us. You've become all there is*
to become: the mocking, blissful smile of an addict
who's half here, nods off on a stoop in a miniskirt,
understanding too well the perpetual voyage then suddenly
jolts up to greet cars sparkling like sin, slowing to a stop

while her daughter upstairs puts both hands under her chin
amused for years, watching a flickering stream of endless images.
And always I call a taxi or pack my rental
and inaudibly say *no*, recalling afternoons
my eyes rarely veered from a book,
even while walking one day from middle school
when a boy lunged a fist in my stomach
like a question mark. I was already awake,
a surfeit of ambition struck: to roam
like decomposing clouds rolling deep,
re-forming constantly and away, above
toughened streets, above sunlit ruins
and scattering mounds. My eyes went
elsewhere or nowhere, open and determined.

Two

Roll on, thou deep and dark blue ocean—Roll!

—GEORGE GORDON BYRON

Urban Renewal

XXI. GREECE

The Cyclades Blues Suite / i.

On the *Aegean Speed Line*, hightailing a fast ferry
away from Perseus's birthplace, away from those beaches
with names like *Ganema, Sykamia, Megalo Livadi*,
whose scythe-like coves left us speechless
and shockingly bold as we unpeeled our bathing suits
like human wrappers, letting pebbly sand stick
to our backs, while the sun conducted its trade routes.
We ask: *Why are we departing again?* Homesick
we are not, though we did wish our three sons
here, so as to astonish that *we* were the better
parents, and surely I cursed the island for its urchins
who fired missiles when my hand sought treasures
near their spiky orbs. I understand now why
children and the dead are abandoned: heaven is a cult
of the irrational. In my glazed-over eyes, your body
found an ally; I rubbed sunscreen until the tumult
in our lives cured right on the spot. Now on deck,
an illness returns. Paradise dwindles to a speck.

ii.

Never get used to this: the morning slow prayer of palm
leaves, feisty light caressing the cubed
halls on the hills in the Chora, the mewling psalms
of homeless cats, surf roiling its evaporating tubes;
salute the snails climbing in clusters like Salgado's miners
up the stalk of some flower, since what you grieve is not
the sublime change of seasons, but the major
hurts you caused in loving too many women. That hot
orb dazzles the heart to a spectacle but you've one more
chance to focus like the Greek sparrow balanced
on the precipice of a roof, nest matter in his mouth
looking for a moment to the shore, then like a lance
taking flight to build a home. Never get used to this:
yucca leaves lifting like a chorus of arms,
the garnishing blue of the Aegean Sea splitting
your eyes into a million sparkling charms.

iii.

Every island is filled with loneliness, even Serifos,
where a donkey's eye is a suffering despondent,
where Father Makarious makes the sign of the cross
as waves arrive like faithful correspondents
and tamarisk trees tender shade like floating coins
and a fisherman slaps his octopus again and again
on a stone by the bay of Livadi at dawn,
and the dazzling nipples of Americans redden
to rusted dials, sharing one sun, where one may take
such signs as nature's camaraderie, except that waitress
who cuts her listless eyes so deep she stakes
you to that label *tourist*, as though excess were the body's
supply at every given place, especially at night
when studded lights mend the horizon where cars zigzag
terraced mountains, and what's heard are voices blown
for thousands of years over villas beyond sagebrush
that bears your grief so familiar you weep.

XXII. SPAIN

La Barraca Blues Suite / i.

for Mark Strand

Beneath canopies of green, unionists marched doggedly
outside *The Embassy*. Their din was no match
for light lancing through leaves of madrone trees
lining the Paseo then flashing off glossy black *Maybachs*
skidding round a plaza like a monarch fleeing the paparazzi.
Your voice skipped and paused like a pencil.
Layers of morning pastries flaked gingerly
then fell, soft as vowels, on a china plate. One learns
to cherish the wizened reserve of old world manners,
two blotched hands making wings of a daily paper
beside us between sips of café con leche, a demeanor
in short gentle as grand edifices along this boulevard.
Yet *Guernica* is down the street, and some windshields
wear a sinister face, sometimes two. Think Goya. Just south
of here, on the lower slopes of the Sierras, fields
of olive groves braid the land like a Moorish head, but
those sultans were kicked out long ago. In the lobby
of the *Hotel Urban*, I wait for a cab, my obedient rolling bag
like a pet beside me. I have loved again another city
but Madrid is yours: her caped *olé*'s, her bullish flag,
her glass pavilions and outdoor tables like a festival
of unbroken laughter, our dark harbors, finding level.

ii.

Salobreña

That stretch of mountains features white windmill
blades whose slow turns are rifles aiming, for I cannot
help but think of Lorca's killing between here and the
   village
Alfaçar, and the firing squad's gun pops are that Flamencan
dancer's heel stomps. I bring back, too, her brisk hand claps
and the cantor's Andalusian moans like dried sticks,
or bones crumbling in his throat. Only souvenir shops
and steep winding streets accrete in this region's stacked
brochures. Her dress spills across the restaurant's floor
like a red shadow, darker than billboards of black bulls
high above roadways, motionless but seeming to gallop
like Franco's brigades. All seeing is an act of war.
Tanks and artillery or Spanish castles and mosques?
I choose to lose, and beneath a watercolorist's sky
study Didi's splendor, nude against the unruffled backdrop
of the Alboran Sea whose waves match my sighs
and bomb this beach, launching sprays of white duds.

iii.

Córdoba, Mezquita

Even if he'd pulled over to study Andalusia's road signs,
after one thousand and one nights, he still could
not make out its calligraphic script, its vertical lines,
its dots, marks like smoke stilled from incense, its curled
sand soft Arabic, but this city's voice has coffins
and carnations, and its hoarse singing shoots through him
like twelve bars of earthen road that lengthens
into a labyrinth of knowing blood beneath black skin.
More echoes: the Alhambra sent him back to the seraglio
of his youth where a Moorish guard stood in a museum,
unfazed by a harem's rising laughter behind palace doors.
Here are pillars and banded arches to once again
imagine the body passing through like a key into infinity.
Was this the answer to his ghetto past? But why travel
so far? Since a child, even in sleep, he voyaged and broke free,
tossing dice in dreams, once below deck on a caravel
next to grains of paradise. He's collecting a thousand faces.
He's moving beneath eyelids, turning time into flesh.
Don't judge him. The courtyard's orange trees where once
he washed like a morisco are teaching his tongue the craft.

XXIII. BRAZIL

Berimbau

You, bow-shaped recipe of opulent whines
on steel wire, who keeps the buzz on an acrobat's spine,
or in a circle, open-aired against the city's noise, or
silent in a studio—at night especially—before
a bustling round of capoeiristas' flying kicks, strike
me a pageant of notes and tell how the snake
wriggles free its skin, how bones laid at a door
curses him who crosses a sill, how in Congo Square
on Sundays, African dances kept six hundred slaves alive,
how war defines a century, how the last goodbye
is often a surprise, how the silver bars of a ladder
means someone needs setting free, or sadder
still, how we must always answer *Who are we?*: that is,
we're set upon by gourd & stone; you're the crisis
I hear when I bend to kiss my son, or when,
at a bar standing, see my brown face in a glass of rum.

XXIV. KENYA

The Dadaab Suite / i.

The UN Somali driver speeds by a small herd
of white cattle prodded along by a desert farmer.
Rust-colored dust in its wake clouds barbed-
wire suburbs of white tents and makeshift shelters
of twigs and branches breeding the plateau faster
than malarial flies. I have come to Dadaab like an actor
on a press release, unprepared for the drained faces
of famine-fleeing refugees, my craft's glamour
dimmed by hundreds of infant graves, children
whose lolling heads' final drop landed on their mothers'
backs like soft stones. What beauty can I spell in
this swelter of dust? Ridged like that farmer's
goats, the ribs of others protrude and make a mockery
of my pen. Where is my empathy? The drought
is in my heart as well as on their skins. Yesterday, I walked
the Maasai Mara and saw how nature bears out
its designs: hyenas drew near for the attack; seconds
later, the sound of crushing bones racked my ears;
a battalion of lions gorged on a half-eaten gazelle.
Two nonchalant giraffes glided by like war profiteers.

ii.

Security Briefing

As you can see the camps are overpopulated,
and the small parts in between, if somebody
vanishes, getting to them is like a reunion date
that never goes down. In rain, roads are too muddy,
at all times too narrow. UN police are afraid
of patrolling in between on crowded footpaths
because you never know who will shoot you, what laid
plans will ambush your breath. There's no moth's
flickering because there's no lighting system
at night. So it becomes quite a dangerous place.
So far, my security has not had to face a similar
plight, but the risk is there. The other possible case
that you are looking at is the threat of hostage
taking. We now have confirmed the presence
of Raskamboni, Al-Shabaab, TFG, the offstage players
who snatch refugees then vanish quick as a scent.

iii.

Child Soldier

When they came to camp, they asked my friend Abdi
if he was ready to join the militia. He said, no.
We were on a crowded matatu to Dagahaley.
The van was loud with voices overflowing;
still I heard one say Shabaab would give Abdi dollars.
I was already thinking it would be fun to play
war, to soldier tough, walk with an AK.
I used to get beat in the market. The harder
I fought, the more they'd gang up.
But U.S. cash would buy more than respect;
I would take care of my sisters. My father
every day tells me I need to do more than sit
my life away.
        Before we reached the border,
they gave us uniforms and said we were now
Allah's warriors. We had to tow ammunition.
They turned us into cattle, into human plows.
We laid mines and roadside bombs. We cleaned guns
as big as us. There were other boys near
my age. With them, I felt among brothers
I never had—one, my best friend Kassim, sixteen, a year
older. Sometimes in the afternoon, we played soccer.

iv.

We kicked for the same team. We prayed
next to each other on sajjada during salat.
Shabaab saw this and gave me a new gun and said
I must shoot Kassim. Now and then, they do this
to test our trust.
                          I see him in my dreams.
He talks! Wonders why. I killed him for
nothing. I sleep. I cry. I thought Allah the Supreme,
the merciful, would have us love the war
with infidels, not my friends. I had to escape.
I wanted back home, god willing, with my mother
and my sisters. So while others slept, one night I draped
and ran the desert. Allah guided me further.
I did not stop, and he helped me to brave
bandits and hyenas. I walked a full day and a half
before a pickup truck braked and hissed to a halt. A grave
silence all the way to camp. No one smiled. No laughs
for a new beginning, just the exhausted looks of terror
and fear and hunger, just the awful smell of vomit
and urine, a collection of faces like smoking embers.

v.
Of

Of enemies, of men surrounding women
and the countless rapes fifteen miles
from the border, even on the outskirts around
camps, how those women speak little, their smiles
like broken carts, of villagers who though alive,
their skin smells like carcasses of dead goats
and sheep, of the sweet rage that grows in desert
flowers, how they pause when their children sleep,
of arriving here, children dying on long walks,
of sons taken from homes and shot in Somali streets,
of gestures and dimming eyes but no words
and no poems and no news bites, of hugs goodbye
and feeling in the body a lost brother to rifle fire,
of yellow jerrycans in a woman's hands,
of women whose walk and sighs in the market
tell of red sand and breathing while counting the hours,
of scavenging storks, of horrors seething
at dusty checkpoints on earth, of a clarity torqued
so high it burns the face, so that when you head home,
lifting up and away from the airstrips' macadam
rippling dry heat, rising back to a mountainous land
whose green hurts to look, of chest drums
like a warning, of your eyes flooding to a monsoon.

vi.

Tour of the Food Distribution Point, Ifo

Over a tundra of red sand they arrive eager as stadium
fans with laundry-like sacks and bags separated into queues:
men and women awaiting the globe's provisions.
I try not to look at their silt-soft eyes, but to parade through
marks us and them as exotic as snow monkeys in Central
Park. The clichéd view begs the clichéd question:
Who is on display? The observer or the observed? A heckle
begins from a shawled woman in the crowd, then the mock rerun
of *One Flew Over the Cuckoo's Nest*; they ululate
and chant till their high-pitched tongue trills turn the warehouse
to a dark forest. Our stage fright is sudden; we hurry straight
to the shed and scrutinize as the flour scooper shows
how the frontlines of hunger are shortened by a white
pour into the *Heart of Darkness*. They wait for the First
of the Month like the poor in Detroit, a flea bite solution
in the fight against famine. We're stuck, our roles rehearsed.

vii.
Security Briefing

Another main concern or risk that we face apart
from civil unrest is the threat of banditry,
mainly between Dadaab and Liboi, by far
the most menacing quandary,
all the way to the border areas and now
like a skirt of cancer around the camps. Last Friday,
for example, a group of young bandits scowling
like a covey of warlords in trucks went to Dagahaley,
to one of the blocks. You know what a block
looks like? Well they took forty-five minutes,
robbing door to door with their glocks
and AK bayonets. If you tried
to scream they break your bit with it, blood
on the buttstock. By the time police realized,
after phone calls were made, they out
already. On Saturday, again, in Dagahaley,
the same guns robbed five shops in a row.
In the markets there, did their robbing and they
disappear, a mirage on the distant plateau.

viii.

In the placid lean of an arid summer, in the lingering
snarl of pit latrines, the sharp barbs of the acacia
thorn tree, in the opaque eyes of the girl fingering
frenziedly her arm's badge of skin suffering cholera,
unearth a feeling for a people who are not your own,
in the sinister look of the man beneath a koofiyad
(he is not al-Shabaab), in the boy selling refurbished phones
in the market, wary of your presence, your queries, the aloof
gaze of women behind hijabs who flee
your camera's barrel, who swiftly turn and cover,
in this land devoid of vegetation like a dried sea
that stretches to their war-torn country scarred over
like a child soldier's back. The camps swell in singeing heat,
hot as empty air of eyeless politicians who have no stake
in other clans. Embrace the father who chews khat,
the girl who sells her limbs for all her body can take.
Think of the rootless, the dispersed, when you slide
into the porcelain glove of your tub like an emperor,
call back the Horn of Africa. Close the divide.
For fear of despair's reprisal, pray they love in return.

XXV. ITALY

The Augustan Suite / i.
for Derek Walcott

> The blessed will not care what angle
> they are regarded from. —W. H. AUDEN

Cobbled streets have the burnished look of stone skulls
sinking like a necropolis of Ugolinos from centuries
of bewildered tourists stumped in the Eternal City, mulling
over which way to turn. Every ruin begets a selfie
like a Hollywood set directed to life then ditched
with each phone's shutter click. Past the bronzed
façade of the Colosseum, ominous as a chipped gold tooth,
other crowds follow like apostles the voice of a guide, yawning
and carrying her flag aloft like a cross. Even here I look for
a history of myself. In the *Musei Vaticani*, I zoom close
to Art's record: frescoes, sculptures, altarpieces, and war
with pilgrims for the best shot, studying the prose
of a guidebook to explain Exekias's amphora,
the slave boy delivering clothes to a nude Pollux,
or why every Christ child craves the adoration of a
black Magus: *shades frozen in a single hole.*
The crumbling stone beneath our feet speaks to us;
even Rome's dust possesses something of human
grandeur, the elegance of decay. I envy the triumph
that certain paintings give back my face, but *Romanus
Pontifex* almost sealed my fate. I have more hills to climb.
From every gift shop, Papa waves at his blessed lambs.

ii.

The Great Beauty

One evening someone will dream of Tuscany and see us
walking along a narrow country road past Relais
San Bruno, plum-littered, beside the north-facing slopes
of vines like formations of green soldiers on their way
to nowhere, a stray dog trotting ahead like Hecuba
who halts and impatiently looks back, checking
our progress to San Biagio. If dreams are rumors,
we are sliding into the light of prayer, practicing
soliloquies of silence in our first year of marriage,
our astonishment punctuated by those cypresses
whose exclamations put a point to blessings. Offstage,
if that sleeper should change pose, and half undress
herself of sheets, let her shift not break cataclysmic
and lose sight of the stone-bright travertine walls,
nor the hills rolling soft as her body, these ancient brick
farmhouses, nor morning's rustic tinkling call
of sheep bells, the honeyed fortress of this city whose blush
of red poppies in fields below collapses some tourist,
our dreamer, into the arms of her husband, crushed
by the view from Montepulciano, nor the way she holds his
hand against her chest lost in a pasture of tiny dwellings
whose faith repeats in campaniles that reach her deepest wells.

iii.

We must be rooted in the absence of place.

—SIMONE WEIL

That window at the Grand Hotel Palazzo in Livorno
framed the Tyrrhenian Sea like a white-bordered postcard
he placed gently on an imaginary wire rack below
other views accruing whose postmarks
he'd yet to stamp, so they swiveled in his mind
involuntarily and slowed with a squeak: perched angels
standing guard on the bridge of Sant'Angelo, the crenelated line
of cliffs above some coast, a shop owner waving farewell,
a series of roundabouts whose circles he never
completed, the half-erect heads of sunflowers like a cavalry
in training, all clichés of travel, even the waterfront *terrazza*
with its checkerboard squares. But not her pillowed beauty
still sunk in sleep, a soft coating of night sweat on her face,
her neck lengthening into a Modigliani. The arrowing flashes
of fallen stars he prayed upon were superfluous; their places
changed, but she, she would remain like the horizon whose light
increased, flooding their rented room. Dawn arrived, the shrieking
seagulls circled into view, next, a ferry, launched to fulfill its routes.
Flip this over, a scene scrawled in lines clear as Greek, stealthily
composed then slipped under his door like a hotel receipt.

Three

Thy kindred echoes roll;

Deep calling unto deep

—AMY CLARKE, "CAERDYN"

ON DISAPPEARING

I have not disappeared.
The boulevard is full of my steps. The sky is
full of my thinking. An archbishop
prays for my soul, even though
we met only once, and even then, he was
busy waving at a congregation.
The ticking clocks in Vermont sway

back and forth as though sweeping
up my eyes and my tattoos and my metaphors,
and what comes up are the great paragraphs
of dust, which also carry motes
of my existence. I have not disappeared.
My wife quivers inside a kiss.
My pulse was given to her many times,

in many countries. The chunks of bread we dip
in olive oil is communion with our ancestors,
who also have not disappeared. Their delicate songs
I wear on my eyelids. Their smiles have
given me freedom which is a crater
I keep falling in. When I bite into the two halves
of an orange whose cross-section resembles my lungs,

a delta of juices burst down my chin, and like magic,
makes me appear to those who think I've
disappeared. It's too bad war makes people
disappear like chess pieces, and that prisons

turn prisoners into movie endings. When I fade
into the mountains on a forest trail,
I still have not disappeared, even though its green façade
turns my arms and legs into branches of oak.
It is then I belong to a southerly wind,
which by now you have mistaken as me nodding back
and forth like a Hasid in prayer or a mother who has just
lost her son to gunfire in Detroit. I have not disappeared.

In my children, I see my bulging face
pressing further into the mysteries.

In a library in Tucson, on a plane above
Buenos Aires, on a field where nearby burns
a controlled fire, I am held by a professor,
a general, and a photographer.
One burns a finely wrapped cigar, then sniffs
the scented pages of my books, scouring
for the bitter smell of control.
I hold him in my mind like a chalice.
I have not disappeared. I swish the amber
hue of lager on my tongue and ponder the drilling
rigs in the Gulf of Alaska and all the oil-painted plovers.

When we talk about limits, we disappear.
In Jasper, TX you can disappear on a strip of gravel.

I am a life in sacred language.
Termites toil over a grave,
and my mind is a ravine of yesterdays.
At a glance from across the room, I wear

September on my face,
which is eternal, and does not disappear
even if you close your eyes once and for all
simultaneously like two coffins.

MIGHTY PAWNS

If I told you Earl, the toughest kid
on my block in North Philadelphia,
bow-legged and ominous, could beat
any man or woman in ten moves playing white,
or that he traveled to Yugoslavia to frustrate the bearded
masters at the Belgrade Chess Association,
you'd think I was given to hyperbole,
and if, at dinnertime, I took you
into the faint light of his Section 8 home
reeking of onions, liver, and gravy,
his six little brothers fighting on a broken love-seat
for room in front of a cracked flat-screen,
one whose diaper sags it's a wonder
it hasn't fallen to his ankles,
the walls behind doors exposing sheetrock
the perfect O of a handle, and the slats
of stairs missing where Baby-boy gets stuck
trying to ascend to a dominion foreign to you and me
with its loud timbales and drums blasting down
from the closed room of his cousin whose mother
stands on a corner on the other side of town
all times of day and night, except when her relief
check arrives at the beginning of the month,
you'd get a better picture of Earl's ferocity
after-school on the board in Mr. Sherman's class,
but not necessarily when he stands near you
at a downtown bus-stop in a jacket a size too
small, hunching his shoulders around his ears,

as you imagine the checkered squares of his poverty
and anger, and pray he does not turn his precise gaze
too long in your direction for fear he blames
you and proceeds to take your Queen.

DREAMS OF PERMANENCE
after William Cordova

How many times have I driven past
and not noticed the beauty of the abandoned
truck, its black-tinted windows safeguarding
a homeless man's makeshift bed, or taken in
that war of names, the faint, illegible,
legible scribblings dashed off in weak light
of a nearby lamppost just before city cops,
seemingly patrolling only this part of town,
rush to manhandle some shy kid who longs
merely for the miraculous,—a recognition unfound
among his six younger siblings whose sprawling
caretaking fades him to a name among names
when needed & called in their cramped
walk-up apartment? Here, in the open
gallery a lot makes, a canvas for the poor,
this non-erasable truck, a quick aerosol emboss
where he swiftly tattoos and revives each letter
in a made-up name like gold till it glitters even
in darkness on a city with its spilled tires,
crumbling façades, and sidewalks blossoming
weeds, detonating dreams of permanence.
No wonder then, each would-be immortal hasn't
climbed the truck's roof and tagged the upper reaches,
having to scurry their scrawlings fast enough to sign
evidence of having been here: *Dondi, Samo,*
Lee, or *Oz,* then a make on the run.

STAND YOUR GROUND (a double golden shovel)

America, how often I have applauded your flagpoles. We,
as citizens, struggle to find common ground, yet do
much to damage the planks of your Ark. Not
a soft tune we make, glissando of the harmonized. We have a want
problem: more of ourselves problem, *Us* versus *Them*
in the great race to prosperity. In his *Introduction to*
Metaphysics, Heidegger asks "Why are there beings at all?" We have
as guides: Klansmen and eugenicists, who proclaim all others are less.
It is, I admit, the slapping of your ropes tolling a perfect union. But,
is the measure of your worth a silent clang elsewhere? How is it
a ripple also runs through *me* when your wind rises? Your cloth is
nation, hauled down or half-mast, like a deferred dream only
earthly because we strive on a path hidden by dead leaves, a natural
entity whose death makes valid its rebirth,—that
an angry man can shoot a teenager is par, as we say. We,
Iota, Deltas, Crips, Knights, new tribesmen in new codes, should
in earnest put away our swords and talk shows. Think:
our watermelons have so many seeds, and we,
galaxy in us, dissolve our supernovas. The mysteries we have,
an unmitigated burning of sound and fury, not
organism of one, but organs. America, I've had enough.

THINKING OF OUR SHAME AT THE GAS PUMP

After nights of strobe lights spinning
hollow festive moods, after listening
to the vast embroidery of our loneliness
at *Vagabond* or *The G Lounge*,
after pursuing a private pain mornings
on subways heading home as I read Russian
history and pretended to walk among
a grove of winter trees, hoping to elude
the snarling, mangy dogs roaming
the streets between Girard and Fairmont,

I let two kinds of time pass through me
and shunned the dying madness of corners,
idling cars exchanging Franklins
and Jacksons for delicious bags of cocaine
as if all noses were peasants turned Bolsheviks.
If a correct revolution of minds had come,
I was ready to banish all evidence of myself,
to escape the bright spoors of shell-top
Adidas hanging like testes over power lines.

I now find myself unable to stare across
two islands of gas pumps and advertisements
for *Big Gulps* at my neighbors' shame,
the big whooshing wind of petrol cleansing us
like a complex pattern of synthesizers
and drum machines, a composed miracle
from the saints of progress and commerce.

When we pray, our hands carry the scent
of gasoline, which confuse our brains' God spot
like the brutally noble monks who publicly
claimed their end and set themselves aflame
in protest, an act replicated in Richard
Linklater's film *Waking Life*. Yet now,
also my dream: that irascible man
sanctimoniously reasoning society's
craving for chaos and destruction
before dousing himself with a devil-red
gas can, then cross-legged on a street corner,
lighting a match as though he were
taking a bath of fire, his charred limbs
collapsing into a heap of embers.

To the question, "Do you have any last words,"
before being euthanized by injection,
the *New York Times* reported Thomas Youk
as saying, "I never understood a thing,"
and then slumped, his head lolling
to one side like a baby's except forever.

I have friends each year who attend *Burning Man*
in Black Rock Desert. They like having sex
in the semi-arid, alkali flats of northern Nevada,
their bodies blurring to ashes like forty-foot
wooden effigies in a swirling dust, eddying up
and marrying to the vast ritual of ruin
and devastation we seem to have made.

Such public performances, such dissent,
our flailing in discotheques, the bonfire
we make of our bodies is, sure, the irrepressible
blaze of the human, but I read, too, all desire
for meaning abandoned as the flames flare
around us, the startling conclusion
of our perpetual obliviousness.

The islands where we refuel offer temporary
clarity: hose, hole, cap, and go. The shame
we all know is we all leave empty.

Four

My man rocks me, with one steady roll
There's no slippin' when he wants to take hold
—TRIXIE SMITH, "MY MAN ROCKS ME"

OK CUPID

Dating a Catholic is like dating a tribe
    and dating a tribe is like dating a nation
and dating a nation is like dating a football star
    and dating a football star is like dating a new car
and dating a new car is like dating an air freshener
    and dating an air freshener is like dating a fake tree
and dating a fake tree is like dating silver tinsel
    and dating silver tinsel is like dating a holiday
and dating a holiday is like dating a black man
    and dating a black man is like dating a top
and dating a top is like dating a bottom
    and dating a bottom is like dating a Tibetan
and dating a Tibetan is like dating a dragon
    and dating a dragon is like dating a fireplace
and dating a fireplace is like dating a mantel
    and dating a mantel is like dating a picture frame
and dating a picture frame is like dating Martin Luther King with Jesus
    and dating Martin Luther King & Jesus is like dating a threesome
and dating a threesome is like dating a commune
    and dating a commune is like dating an unachievable idea
and dating an idea is like dating the Enlightenment
    and dating the Enlightenment is like dating science
and dating science is like dating a beaker
    and dating a beaker is like dating a pharmacy
and dating a pharmacy is like dating a dealer
    and dating a dealer is like dating a supply chain
and dating a supply chain is like dating a Republican
    and dating a Republican is like dating winter

and dating winter is like dating Demeter
and dating Demeter is like dating corn
and dating corn is like dating pancakes
and dating pancakes is like dating an orgasm
and dating an orgasm is like dating Utopia
and dating Utopia is like dating an Amish woman
and dating an Amish woman is like dating a Luddite
and dating a Luddite is like dating a folk hero
and dating a folk hero is like dating Robert Zimmerman
and dating Robert Zimmerman is like dating history
and dating history is like dating a white man
and dating a white man is like dating insecurity
and dating insecurity is like dating a Hummer
and dating a Hummer is like dating the Pentagon
and dating the Pentagon is like dating a lost star
and dating a lost star is like dating a liberal
and dating a liberal is like dating a Jew
and dating a Jew is like dating a lamp
and dating a lamp is like dating a blonde
and dating a blonde is like dating a Swede
and dating a Swede is like dating *IKEA*
and dating *IKEA* is like dating *Whole Foods*
and dating *Whole Foods* is like dating a yoga instructor
and dating a yoga instructor is like dating an e-reader
and dating an e-reader is like dating a television
and dating a television is like dating a commercial
and dating a commercial is like dating a serial murderer
and dating a serial murderer is like dating Raskolnikov
and dating Raskolnikov is like dating a rationalist
and dating a rationalist is like dating an academic
and dating an academic is like dating a CV

and dating a CV is like dating a white woman
and dating a white woman is like dating a breadline
and dating a breadline is like dating a refugee
and dating a refugee is like dating a Cuban
and dating a Cuban is like dating a propane flame
and dating a flame is like dating a topless jihadist
and dating a jihadist is like dating a femme fatale
and dating a femme fatale is like dating Paris Hilton
and dating Paris Hilton is like dating a tabloid
and dating a tabloid is like dating a Communist
and dating a Communist is like dating cut flowers
and dating cut flowers is like dating infidelity
and dating infidelity is like dating a pool

CALYPSO'S MAGICAL GARDEN
after Romare Bearden

It's bad when a man doesn't
own his dreams, a faint
head full of the scent
of a woman, her special claims

and beguiling herbs arched
in the crevices of his ears
like plugs of gold, his scorched
mind far from wife & kids, tears

turning his eyes to pebbles
splashed by briny waves.
Possessing no firm farewell,
she makes his sex a slave.

No will in her cavern,
no choice to rise up a god
free of the banal pattern:
no leaving her roughshod,

her chocolates scattered,
clutching ardent notes.
Instead, on the immortal ladder
of her limbs, he climbs & dotes:

her braided hair, her bangled
wrists, the garden's chimes,

their afternoon mangled
in bits and chunks of time.

Even the birds, stilled to a silence
by the unannounced show, a man
wearing the crown of the island
until she lets him go.

AUBADE

You could be home, boiling a pot
of tea as you sit on your terrace,
reading up on last night's soccer shot
beneath a scarf of cirrus.

You could be diving headlong
into the waves of Cocoa Beach
or teaching Mao Tse-tung
whose theories are easy to reach.

Or dropping off your dry cleaning,
making the New Americans wealthier,
or mowing your lawn, greening
up, but isn't this healthier?

Just imagine the hours you're
not squandering away,
nor the ant-like minutes frittered
with a tentative fiancé.

Your whole body agrees you'd
rather lie here like a snail
in my arm's crook, nude
and oblivious to all emails.

Yes, it's nearly one o'clock.
But we have more reasons

to kiss, to engage in small talk.
For one, these blissful seasons

are short, & tomorrow is never
insured, so bounce downstairs:
pour us glasses of whatever,
a tray of crackers, Bosc pears,

then let drop your sarong,
the wind high on your skin,
so we can test all day long
the notion of original sin.

SPECIAL NEEDS

Only the skin runs ahead like a spruced-up
dream from which I never awake.
What really exists, no one knows.
In exchange for shook foil,
Hopkins killed the agnostic in him.
I want to kill the polygamist in me.
A sound, a whole sound is never a separation.
A whole sound is an angelic order.
I am most whole in an alley off Market Street
where I pretend to be a sentence
and not a sentiment, a friend to stray
cats and beautiful women. My young cousins only want
hard words and money. If the economy sinks, they will
kill you quicker than a brainwave.
I give my sympathy to the last evangelical.
As long as the body is blaring,
we avoid the straitjackets of conformity.
I am zealous for the taste of my life.
Sometimes, I do not sleep for days.
In the mornings, I rub my hands together
back and forth summoning the angels
away from the orthodoxy of façades.
I reach for the peppershaker
on my spice rack and recall all the pimps
of Chelsea and all the johns on Wall Street.
I see joggers in the street and they remind me
of my most treasured liaisons.

Some men are simply malefic and fall
through your window, wanting to be a part
of something good.

INSCRIPTION

Five gold wash crystal pearls on a wrist.
Her seraph-skin glistening when a spigot is turned off
in the apartment next door, letting out
a rusty squeak. A tabby licks a paw.

An evening dinner of lightning in clouds, the sky's release
of electrical surplus followed by Porchetta
with wilted greens tossed in Arbequina olive oil and lemon.

Layers of clothes topped by her sinamay straw derby hat.
A thin wisp of sheen above his brow.
Until all at once they voicelessly consume
the echoes of all their past.

Possible objects of high regard: stalactites dripping
in a cave, delicately carved tortoiseshell comb,
cambers of her body.

NIGHT STEPS

I'll never forget the wind the corner whispered,
nor the windowed darkness that was more
a frame for the world's high-rise loneliness.
I'll never forget the days we lingered
beneath our fingerprints and how we were
each other's private sacrament.
Brooms and mops hung behind doors
like secret agents. The crooks of our knees
ached from all the praying; our astonished hands
could not keep up, being daydreamers
of water towers and such. What monastery would
welcome such afterimages like those we spoke?
Electric wires over a bus stop, a fly mumbling
and dodging a swatter, a light brown maid smiling
on a bottle of corn syrup. I'll never forget
such sprigs of trembling and honeysuckle
nor other forms of desire: the night steps
of an upright bass or blue-eyeshadow
like slashes beneath my mother's brow.

CRIES & WHISPERS

Each day I forget something, yet happy
I never forget to wake
to the bright corollas of summer
mornings. In the jury box of my bed,
I listen to the counterarguments
of finches and blue jays, cardinals and
the tufted titmice, and the sharp judgment
of the crow, grow to sweet clamors.
In my neighborhood, someone like me
is sitting at a kitchen table taking down notes
between bites of granola and gentle sips
of oolong tea and recording the soap opera
in the trees. The pen is her large
antenna to the mysteries which come
in alternate currents of slapstick
and calamity. She writes away her nights
of emptiness and boredom. We'd be perfect
in a Bergman film, both of us entering into day
seeking the final appearance of things,
bumping around like this. A delivery truck
backs into a driveway. The streets
begin their excited breathing.

ON COCOA BEACH

I am revisiting the idea of Florida, giving my vertebrae
a vacation from all the faded bouquets of urine in New York
and the darkened policies of snow in Vermont.
I am revisiting the idea of my wife's imperial gaze;
her three-cheese quiche and fluted mimosas
are the masters of my mornings.
I am revisiting the idea of lawn furniture.
By late afternoon on Sunday my face blossoms
like a passion of lilies as I admire the spectral grace
of the sandhill crane or am caught lost thinking of Castillo
de San Marcos and the first people Timucua.
I am revisiting the idea of light and laughter and skin,
half-transported by wind. I like to think of myself
beside the crepe myrtle pondering the logos
of palm leaves and the kindnesses of beaches.
You can have your sororities of pain and darkened subways.
I will give myself to the great battles of clouds and surfs.

ODE TO MOUNT PHILO

After avocado-colored inclines,
 after dawdling ascents
  over fern & foliage, after long

trillium gazes and careful steppings
 over outcrops of rocks
  which if not careful could

trip to foil, after delicate trail
 talk of marriages and births,
  dates remembered, and quarrels

squashed, the tentative pace
 of the new in-law, the sure-
  footedness of the long-ago loved,

after stop-offs to catch breath,
 a swig and quaff, to take this much
  in, midway up journey,

this resting place to further
 peaks and crests, after foothold
  and climb, after storm's last

sculpture of fallen trees, You,
 summit of my life, philosophy
  of sky, You, embezzler of breaths

from big and small mouths,
    so that all whisper your spread-out
        tabernacle, a new religion,—

You ritual burst of mountain
    light and sparkling lake
        for which we line up

taking our turns in spawns
    of clicks and screens: panorama
        of foothills like green coats

thrown open, clouds, if only
    we could reach & cup into
        our hands, and below,

a stitched patchwork of land:
    lime-pastured like flattened
        squares of kale. We look.

We marvel at how far
    we traveled through
        emerald, glitter, and beam.

ENCHANTERS OF ADDISON COUNTY

We were more than gestural, close-listening,
the scent of manure writing its waft on the leaves
off Route 22A. By nightfall, our gaze flecked
like loon cries, but no one was up for turnips
nor other roots, not least of which the clergy.
Romanticism has its detractors, which is why
we lined the road with tea-lit luminaries
and fresh-cut lemons. We called it making magic,
then stormed the corners and porches
of general stores, kissing whenever cars idled
at four-way stop signs or sought Grade A maple syrup
in tin containers with painted scenes of horse-drawn
farmers plowing through snow. The silhouetted, rusted
farm equipment gave us the laid-back heaven
we so often wished, and fireflies bequeathed earth stars,
such blink and blank and bunk-a-bunk-bunk.
And of course we wondered if we existed,
and also too, the cows of the ancient pastures,
and the white milk inside our heads
like church spires and ice cream cones.
Even after all of that cha-cha-cha, we still came
out of swimming holes shivering our hearts out.

Five

When worst comes to worst,

My peoples come first.

—MOBB DEEP

SELF-PORTRAIT AS THE ALLEGORY OF POETRY

A corpse snores in morning traffic.
I edge along a sidewalk
hoisting trash can after trash can.
Even maggots marvel
at the eloquence of my lift.

I peer inside the roar
of a steel mouth
& know lampshades once
channeled light.
Everyone is dumbstruck

like Cousteau at seaside.
A cat smarter than me
circles a boom box.
An unclothed doll
prostrate on a curb
tans in the sun.

When I lie down at night
my wife says I reek
of recycled news. I carry
wet onions into sleep.
Days unfold in sheaves.

I've pondered retiring
to a shopping cart,

to crushed cans for shoes.
I'd whistle songs only
from my youth.

PATHETIC FALLACY

Jog through this suburb at a blue hour
when bliss blows over dewy lawns
and neighbors walk suspicious dogs
inhaling trunks of oaks and birches
like a posse of pet detectives, and roused
yet cautious, the first mourning dove sings.

Ponder your existence, which someday will
no longer animate the world of creatures
and aviaries.

Could your limbs survive without always
naming the flawless cathedrals of leaf-branches
entwining above your head?

Isn't this what you meant by truly living?
Do you believe it?
Did you mistreat the vowels?

When did you begin to speak, you who love
the grace of a fireplace, its ash
the aftermath of a desperate battle?

You, too, were trying to recover
the myth of Philomela in your own time,
in your own district, in a tenement
built for the wounded and discontent.

Those early days you lived in shadows,
speechless from what you could not name,
yet its absence ever present and growing in
a field peopled by your metaphoric propositions.

You turn onto Circle Drive—a dragonfly
inspects the dark city of your head.

FUNDAMENTALS

When all that we see is all that we hear,
and the blossoming fury of the preacher
in his pulpit thundering down fists
as though your flat screen were a smithy,

but his last name is Dollar, and you listen to
what dat mouf do, a myth dispersion,
enchanting shadow that is romance incarnate.
At first, as though exploding shards
of glass you had passed on your way
to the kitchen in your raspberry beret,
smelling faintly of that which night produces.
But what crept on you, that sense of shame,
which forges its own spring of believers.

The camera cuts to an angled view
of not quartersawn pews but blue, first-class
seats, *praise him*'s and *amen*'s. Half your
life's work is dodging, a self-built home
to get to. So, you walk on, and pass your areca
palm tree and terrarium of golly pods
but not before you lift your remote
and gun down its quiet laser.

CANON OF PROPORTIONS

How unnatural the body cattle-ranched, and yet one feels one's
laughter
seeping
like an unplanned gunfight, zigzagging a queue only to pause
for two
seconds
in a full-on, arms up, frozen jumping jack when the scanner half-
circles
and
backscatters one's genitals, ionizing into a potentially dangerous
phantom.
Thomas
Jefferson was never a frequent flier, and I wonder if the prominent activist
whom I
stand behind
at Reagan International contemplating adult things like climate change,
and executive
orders, ever
deployed a furtive power fist above his head. At this hour, the safety of a
nation
requires
I abandon explosive shoes and double-shot lattes, and model my best
Vitruvian
Man.
It is either this or lonely rail yards. I choose the amateur in the skies
like I choose
a right knee

in prayer. Still it must be said: the occasional lament of a train is an unremembered
dream
and arousal might lead to a pat-down, a telltale pistol of flesh to grieve.

ENERGY LOVES HERE

Sun Ra and His Black Magic Soul Power Arkestra, 2014

Clumsily, so In,
those squares—
such states
of Normalcy,

never to feel
the infinite number
of vibratory ratios.
What I play:

Moonwords for
posterity, north
by Northwest
of the Sea of

Fecundity.
Let me find
Beings like myself
lurking in the

Between-ness
of the Kingdom
of Not. All
creations

are music, the
hopeless retelling:

freedom's birth.
Far clouds

like a face,
and each face
an expedition
in sonic justice.

Go on: play your
mug. Make the boom
boom of the New Thing
where a clock is a crime.

Space is not
your death's cave,
but the lights
turned out in

your mind.
If you stand in
the light of an
interplanetary

church, tenderest
effigy of yourself,
then you, too, can
spar with meteors

or memory. Blow
back the ordinary

jive of planet
Earth: my being

is Beingness,
myth business
like man; every
beginning is

a trauma.
Other Planes
of There we seek:
loss as a kind

of predestination.
In the blades of grass,
mourning. I lie
on midnight's

back, conjuring
equations, hoping
some ear decodes
the rhythmic

figures, futuristic
sounds, outer
darkness music,
black music

orbiting your
neoclassical beam

waves. How is
your life art if

you keep playing easy-
listening inside your
tomb? Asymmetrical
deviations?

When Angels
Speak of Love,
primitive What's
and How's,

the research
and treatment
of cosmic voids.
We aliens have

little memory
which isn't
reality but the
spacecraft

you know as Life.
What it is? Ultra
Beings in the Space
Gallery, I reach

for your feelings
not your brains.

I don't care who
you are, but what

you can be. Man
is limited. This
is celestial
communication

success. Go on.
Walk Across
the Void. Spaceport
Spirit Sound.

WHY I WRITE POETRY

Because my son is as old as the stars
Because I have no blessings
Because I hold tangerines like orange tennis balls
Because I sit alone and welcome morning across
        the unshaved jaws of my lawn
Because the houses on my street sleep like turtles
Because the proper weight of beauty was her eyes
        last night beneath my eyes
Because the red goblet from which I drank
        made even water a Faustian toast
Because radishes should be banned, little pellets
        that they are
Because someone says it's late and begins to rise from a chair
Because a single drop of rain is hope for the thirsty
Because life is ordinary unless you plan
        and set in motion a war
Because I have not thanked enough
Because my lips moisten whenever I hear Mingus's
        "Goodbye Pork Pie Hat"
Because I've said the word dumbfuck too many times in my life
Because I plant winter vegetables in July
Because I could say the morning died like candle wax
        and no one would question its truth
Because I relished being sent into the coatroom
        in third grade where alone, I would turn off the light
        and run my hands over my classmates' coats
        as if playing tag with their bodies
Because once I shoplifted a pair of Hawaiian shorts

and was caught at the Gallery Mall.
Because soup reminds me of the warmth
     of my grandmother and old aunts
Because the long coast of my dreams is filled
     with saxophones and poems
Because somewhere someone is buying a Rolex or a Piaget
Because I wish I could speak three different languages
     but have to settle for the language of business
     and commerce
Because I used to wear paisley shirts and herringbone
  sports jackets
Because I better git it in my soul
Because my grandfather loved clean syntax,
     cologne, Stacy Adams shoes, Irish tweed caps,
     and women, but not necessarily in that order
Because I think the elderly are sexy
     and the young are naïve and brutish
Because a vision of trees only comes to
     wise women and men who can fix old watches
Because I write with a pen whose supply of ink
     comes from the sea
Because gardens are fun to visit in the evenings
     when everyone has put away their coats and swords
Because I still do not eat corporate French fries or rhubarb jam
Because punctuation is my jury and the moon is my judge
Because my best friend in fourth grade chased
     city buses from corner to corner
Because his cousin's father could not stop looking
     up at the sky after his return from the war
Because parataxis is just another way of making ends meet
Because I have been on a steady diet of words
     since the age of three.

NOTES

1. *Reverse Voyage* is inspired by the poetry of Larry Levis.
2. *The Cyclades Blues Suite* is dedicated to Aliki Barnstone.
3. *Salobreña* is dedicated to Garrett Hongo.
4. *Aubade* is an imitation of Richard Wilbur's "Late Aubade."
5. *Stand Your Ground* is a double golden shovel which uses a line from Robert Hayden's "American Journal" and one from Gwendolyn Brooks's "Beverly Hills, Chicago."

ABOUT THE AUTHOR

Major Jackson is the author of four collections of poetry: *Roll Deep* (W. W. Norton, 2015), *Holding Company* (W. W. Norton, 2010), *Hoops* (W. W. Norton, 2006), and *Leaving Saturn* (University of Georgia Press, 2002), which was awarded the Cave Canem Poetry Prize and was a finalist for the National Book Critics Circle Award in Poetry. He is the editor of Library of America's *Countee Cullen: Collected Poems*. Major Jackson is a core faculty member at the Bennington Writing Seminars and the Richard A. Dennis Professor at the University of Vermont. He serves as the poetry editor of the *Harvard Review*.